Contents

The Wareham Bears, Dorset

Elizabeth is a new baby.

Elizabeth has a new teddy bear.

Gran bought teddy the day Elizabeth was born.

New teddies feel soft.

WHOSE WASHING MACHINE IS ALSO A CREDA TUMBLE DRYER?

Drying clothes in a British climate is no teddy bear's picnic. But with the power of electricity and the genius of Creda's Living Technology, every day can be a drying day with a Creda Supaspeed washer dryer.

It handles a substantial 7lb load from wash to dry. It has a final warm rinse to give quicker, more efficient drying and so offer maximum economy.

It has a washing quality that never varies, but spin speeds that do. With Superfast at 1150 rpm for faster drying, or 600 rpm for delicates.

There's no hanging around wet washing with a Supaspeed. There's no hanging around waiting for it to finish either. You can get into the dryer at any time because there is no annoying time lock on the door.

Why buy two appliances when you can do the job in the space of one? Look into a Creda Supaspeed washer dryer before you leap into buying just a washing machine.

For full details and for your DryElectric leaflet send in the coupon or phone 01-200 0200 and ask for DryElectric with Creda.

Electricity and Creda. Making life more bearable.

When they get dirty they go
in the washing machine.

Sarah has lots of teddies.

Some are new.

Some are old.

Here's Sarah with her Mum, Sally.

Sally has her teddy bear.

He's the oldest bear.

He's as old as Sally.

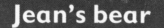

Jean's bear is quite old too.

His fur has come out.

He feels hard, not soft.

You can't wash Jean's bear in the washing machine.

When Jean was young, teddy was a new bear.

Look at him in this picture.

Teddy is the same age as Jean.

Here's a much older bear.

He's nearly eighty years old.

Look at his long arms and pointed snout.

Inside he's full of sawdust and feels very hard.

1911 German bear dressed as a World War I sailor

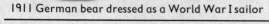

These old bears
are clockwork
bears.

This bear rides
on roller skates.

German, Bing, 1920

Can you see a key to turn?

The two bears walk
if you turn the key.

German, Schuco, c. 1909

Here is one of the oldest bears ever made.

Very old bears are more like real bears.

Rare Steiff Bear, c. 1905

They have humps on their backs,
long arms and tiny black eyes.

Some even make a growling noise.

Some bears have stories written about them.

Alan Alexander Milne with his son Christopher Robin, 1926

This dad wrote a story about this bear.

The bear's name was 'Pooh Bear'.

The first 'Paddington Bear' was bought from a London shop.

All the new 'Paddington Bears' are copied from the first one.

Sketch for 'The House at Pooh Corner' by Ernest Howard Shepard, 1928

Pauline works in a museum.

She looks at lots of old bears.

Some are soft.
Some are hard.

Some have long arms.
Some have short arms.

Some can growl.

Pauline uses these clues
to tell her how old each bear is.

One class took their bears to school.

Some belonged to them.

Some belonged to their Mums and Dads.

One even belonged to a Grandma.

The Teddy Bear Museum, Stratford-upon-Avon

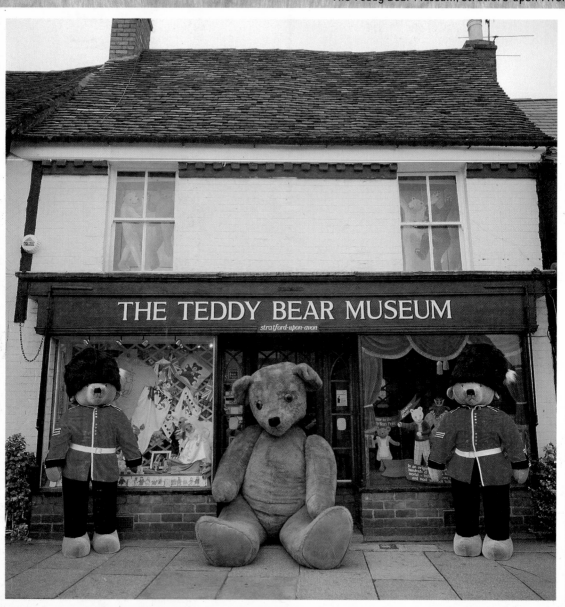

Why not make a museum in your school?

Or go and visit one?